MINECRAFTER

ARCHITECT

THE BUILDER'S IDEA BOOK

MEGAN MILLER

Sky Pony Press
New York

Sky Pony Press books may be purchased in bulk at special discounts for sales promotion, corporate gifts, fund-raising, or educational purposes. Special editions can also be created to specifications. For details, contact the Special Sales Department, Sky Pony Press, 307 West 36th Street, 11th Floor, New York, NY 10018 or info@skyhorsepublishing.com.

Sky Pony® is a registered trademark of Skyhorse Publishing, Inc.®, a Delaware corporation.

Visit our website at www.skyponypress.com.

10 9 8 7 6 5 4

Library of Congress Cataloging-in-Publication Data is available on file.

Cover design by Brian Peterson
Cover and interior illustrations by Megan Miller
Book design by Megan Miller

Print ISBN: 978-1-5107-3764-8
E-Book ISBN: 978-1-5107-3769-3

Printed in China

CONTENTS

INTRODUCTION

SOMETIMES YOU WANT TO BUILD, BUT AREN'T SURE what to build. Other times, you know what you want to build, but you're not sure exactly what it should look like. Or you may be almost finished building but want to add something unique to your build.

There are so many options in choosing a build and in building it that you can sometimes get stuck making a decision, waiting for inspiration. Inspiration often comes unexpectedly, but you can help it along. Browsing magazines, looking at real-life builds, and exploring other people's creations are some avenues for getting inspired. The goal of this book is to be another avenue toward getting inspired for *Minecraft* building. There are sample block palettes, building ideas, and examples of types of roofs, windows, columns, entryways, and more. You can copy them exactly or adapt them to make them your own, or they just may inspire you to do it better!

CHAPTER 1
BUILDING IDEAS

IF YOU ARE ITCHING TO BUILD BUT STUCK on what to build, scan these lists of building and structure types to see if any catch your fancy. (Warning: Long lists of ideas like these can sometimes be overwhelming if you are at the beginning of decision making. If that's the case, just take a quick look, forget you looked, and move on to another chapter!) If you see something you're interested in, you can search online for pictures and illustrations that can help inspire you further.

Dwellings

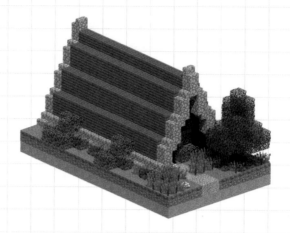

A-frame, adobe home, beach house, bungalow, castle, cave house, chalet, cliff dwellings, cottage, dogtrot house, dugout, earth-sheltered house, farmhouse, hobbit house, houseboat, hovel, igloo, lighthouse, log cabin, longhouse, manor, mansion, palace, pueblo, ranch, roundhouse, shack, stilt house, tent, tipi, trailer, tree house, underground home, villa, yurt

Farm Structures

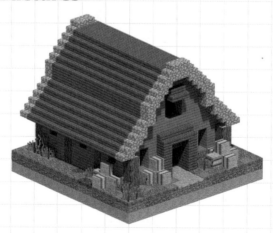

Barn, coop, cow-shed, farmhouse, grain fields, granary, greenhouse, grinding mills, orchards, pig sty, root cellar, shed, silo, stable, water mill, well, windmill, vegetable gardens, vineyard

Medieval Village Structures

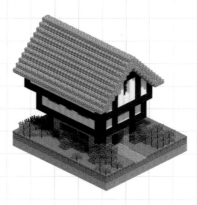

Alms house, bake house, barber, barn, bathhouses, blacksmith, brewery, butcher's, carpenter, charcoal maker, church, cottages, fishery, foundry, furrier, gatehouse, granary, great hall, inn, manor house, market, mason, mill, monastery, parsonage, stables, tailor, tanners, tavern, village green, warehouse, weigh house, well, woodcutter

Town Structures

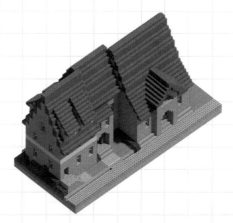

Apartment buildings, art gallery, bakery, bank, bookstore, brewery, car dealership, cinema, city hall, community hall, courthouse, department store, fast food chain, fire station, florist, hospital, hotel, library, museum, office building, plant nursery, police station, post office, prison, pub, restaurants, school, shops, skyscraper, supermarket, swimming pool, theater, townhouse, warehouses, water tower, winery, witches' tower

Infrastructure

Aqueduct, airport, boathouse, bridges, covered bridges, canal, cranes, customs house, dam, dock, garage, hangar, harbors, heliport, highways, lighthouse, paths, ports, quays, railways, railway stations, ranger station, roads, subway (metro), tramway, tunnels, water tower, wharf

Religious Buildings

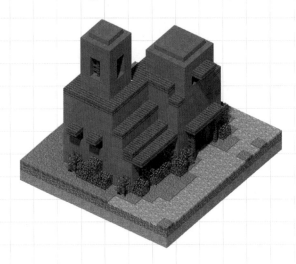

Cathedral, chapel, church, convent, monastery, mosque, pagoda, shrine, synagogue, temple

Animal-Related Structures

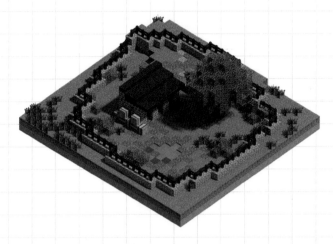

Animal shelter, aquarium, aviary, barn, bat house, chicken coop, corral, cow shed, dog house, kennel, paddock, pig sty, ranch, stables, zoo

Public / Recreational Spaces

Amusement parks, community gardens, fairground, Ferris wheel, fountain, marina, memorial, monument, observation deck, parks, pavilion, pier, planetarium, sports arena, square, stadium, swimming pool, theater, triumphal arch, village green, zoo

Military Structures

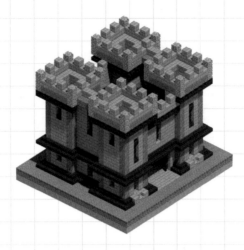

Armory, arsenal, barracks, bunker, castle, citadel, fort, fortification, garrison, guardhouse, installation, military camp, operating base, secret military base, shipyard

Industrial Structures

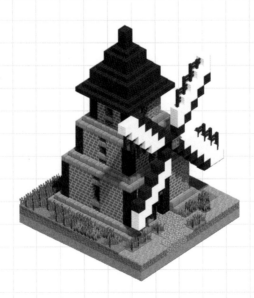

Brewery, distillery, drilling rig, factory, forge, foundry, gristmill, mill, mine, oil and gas platforms, power plant, quarry, sawmill, warehouse, water tower

Miscellaneous Structures

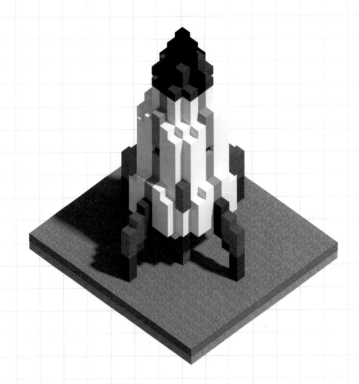

Airplane, arcade, archery range, biosphere, boat, camp, clubhouse, clock tower, folly, graveyard, grotto, jet, maze, pier, pyramid, rocket ship, ship, ski lodge, spa, stone circles, research station, retaining wall, storm cellar, summer camp, tennis court, tower, UFO, water slide, wizard or witches' tower, ziggurat

CHAPTER 2
WINDOWS

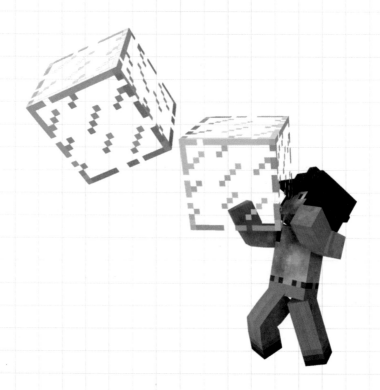

WINDOWS MAY SEEM LIKE A DETAIL TO ADD on to buildings, but really they can be the heart and soul of a building. In real life, windows let you look outside and add patterns of light and shadow inside. They create a relationship between the indoors and the outdoors. While light doesn't behave quite the same way in *Minecraft*, windows do still direct the look and feel of your build. They are a primary way to add detail and depth.

Ways to make your windows stand out include the following:

Use glass panes (almost always) rather than glass blocks

Glass panes add depth to your building because they are inset rather than flush with block edges.

Frames

Add frames around your windows. You can use stairs, slabs, blocks, and more to create a frame and sill. The frame can be in line with the wall or extend out from it. Window frames are a good opportunity to add contrast to your walls: light against dark, bright against dull, textured against smooth. You can place framing around the entire window or just one or more sides.

Contrast

Use contrasting blocks and textures around your windows.

Use alternatives to glass

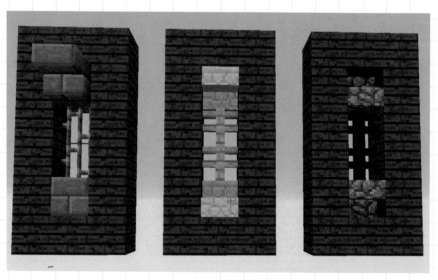

In some builds, like castles and medieval or rustic buildings, fences, and iron bars could be a good alternative to glass.

Inset or extend the window area

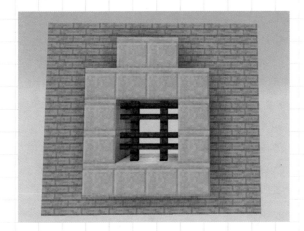

Depending on your build, you may want to inset the entire window area or extend it out from the wall. Simply moving a block away from the building's walls adds depth. You can make the windows two or three blocks deep, using outer and inner framing. You can also add a larger frame or border around the window area.

Use stairs and slabs for patterned openings

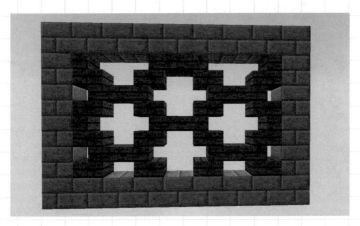

You don't always have to have glass or fences to fill in your windows. You can use stairs and slabs in complicated or simple patterns to create different shapes and openings.

The Right Window for the Job ——

WHEN YOU ARE PLANNING YOUR BUILD, YOU WILL WANT TO THINK ABOUT HOW YOUR WINDOWS WILL WORK INTO YOUR DESIGN. TRADITIONAL "IMPORTANT" BUILDINGS TEND TO HAVE REGULARLY PLACED AND LARGER-SIZED WINDOWS, MODERN DESIGNS MIGHT PLAY AROUND WITH DIFFERENT SIZES AND SHAPES, AND VERNACULAR OR LOCAL ARCHITECTURE MAY HAVE MORE IRREGULAR AND SMALLER WINDOWS. ARCHITECTS ALSO DESIGN AND PLACE WINDOWS TO HIGHLIGHT OR FOCUS ON A SPECIFIC VIEW OR TO CREATE PLEASING AREAS OF LIGHT AND SHADE.

Add eaves or small roofs to windows

You can use stairs and slabs in different positions to create small overhangs for your windows.

Experiment with unusual blocks for detailing

Great blocks for detailing your windows include trap doors, fences, gates, walls, stairs, slabs, carpet, iron bars, ladders, end rods, anvils, and signs. To make shutters, you can use doors as well as trap doors and ladders.

The Belt Course

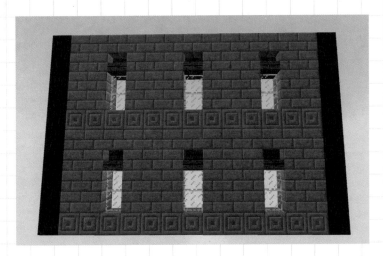

A BELT COURSE IS A DECORATIVE ROW OF STONES OR BRICK THAT RUNS BETWEEN WINDOWS OR FLOORS. YOU CAN USE THEM TO BREAK UP THE FLAT WALL OF A BUILDING.

More Windows

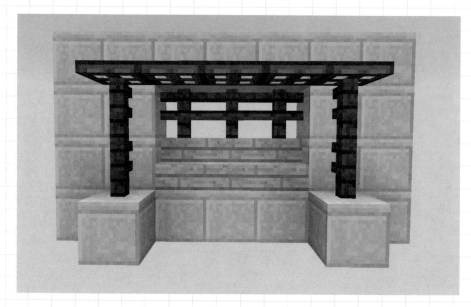

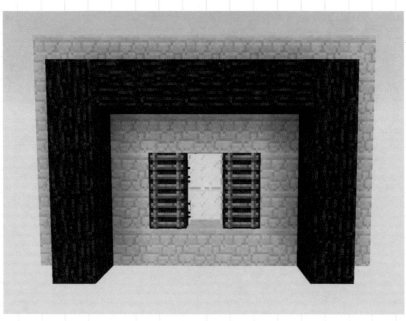

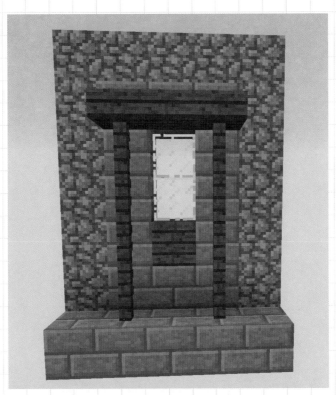

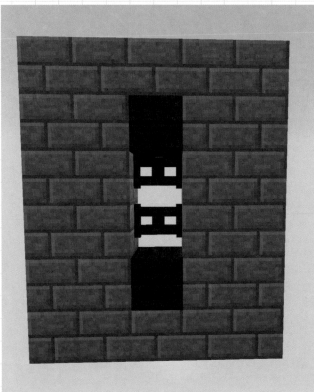

CHAPTER 3
WALLS AND FENCES

WALLS AND FENCES ARE GREAT FOR KEEPING MOBS out of your base. They usually end up being long and flat and featureless, because that is the easiest way to build them. But if you take some time, repeating patterns and adding variety, you can really make your cities, towns, builds, and spaces come alive. Tactics you can use to create unique and interesting walls and fences include the following.

Use posts at regular intervals

You can break up a long, flat wall by placing posts, columns, towers, or fortifications at regular intervals. Even simple columns can add a lot of visual interest to a wall.

Incorporate recesses and extrusions

Recess or extrude portions of the wall to add more depth and interest.

Use multiple layers

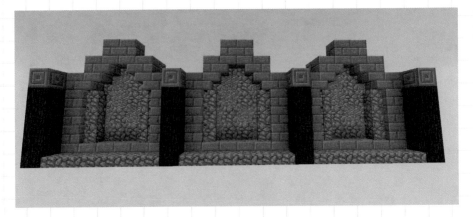

In front of a "base" inner wall, you can place several other layers of wall. Using different blocks, colors, and shapes for the wall will add a lot of visual interest.

Use different colors and textures

You can add.depth and variety to even a flat wall by using blocks that have different textures and colors.

Using gaps to break up solid surfaces

Use slabs, stairs, spaces, walls, iron bars, and fences to create gaps in the wall, letting you see what's beyond the wall or revealing an inner surface.

Use movement

Rather than follow a straight line, make your wall take a few detours. These can be corners and curves to avoid other structures, like farms or boulders or lakes. Have your wall follow the landscape, rising up and lowering as it does. When following the height of the landscape, it's often best to maintain a minimum length of wall that remains at the same height. For example, lower or raise a wall only at its primary columns or posts.

Designing a Wall

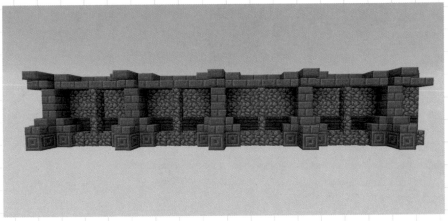

WHEN YOU ARE DESIGNING A WALL, START WITH THE BASIC FORM AND STRUCTURE FIRST: HOW TALL WILL THE COLUMNS BE; HOW ARE THEY SPACED; WHAT ARE THE MAIN MATERIALS OF THE PALETTE? ADD DETAILS OR BLOCKS LIKE STAIRS AND SLABS TO FINISH THE BASE AND TOP OF THE COLUMNS. WHEN YOU LIKE HOW YOUR COLUMNS LOOK, MOVE ON TO DESIGNING THE WALLS BETWEEN THEM.

Detailing

YOU CAN MAKE A CASUAL OR OLD FARM FENCE LOOK WORN AND PARTIALLY CRUMBLING BY USING A COMBINATION OF COBBLESTONE, ANDESITE, AND GRAVEL.

GREAT BLOCKS FOR DETAILING AND ADDING DEPTH TO WALLS INCLUDE TRAP DOORS, BUTTONS, PRESSURE PLATES, FENCES, GATES, WALLS (OF COURSE!), STAIRS, AND SLABS.

More Walls and Fences

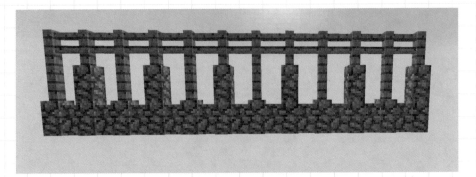

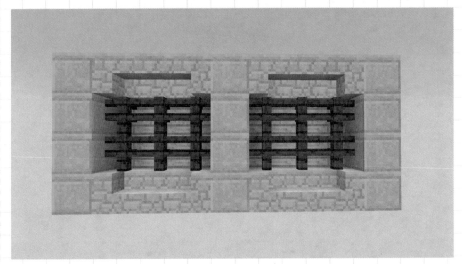

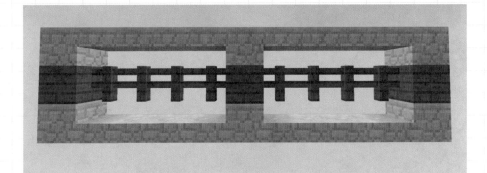

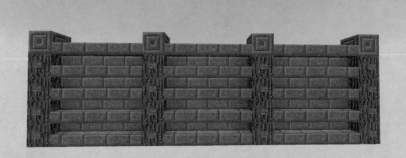

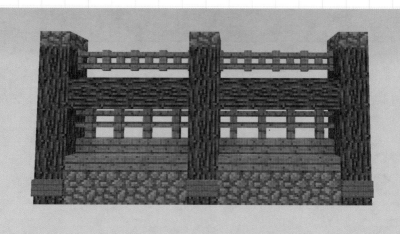

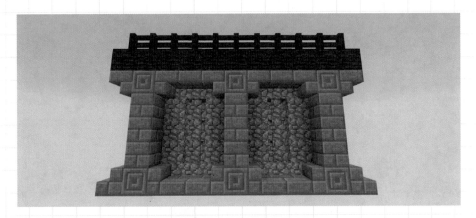

Crumbling Walls

WALLS DON'T ALL HAVE TO BE IN PERFECT SHAPE. YOUR MINECRAFT COUNTRYSIDE AREAS MAY BE BORDERED AND DEFINED BY AGING, CRUMBLING, AND PARTLY MISSING WALLS, HEDGES, AND FENCING. YOU CAN USE BROKEN-UP STRETCHES OF FULL BLOCKS, STAIRS, AND SLABS OF COBBLESTONE, ANDESITE, CRACKED BRICK, AND GRAVEL IN UNEVEN SHAPES, ALONG WITH LEAF BLOCKS AND GRASS, TO SIMULATE ANCIENT BORDER WALLS.

CHAPTER 4
DOORS AND ENTRANCEWAYS

EVEN THOUGH DOORS ARE *MINECRAFT* OBJECTS THAT YOU really cannot change without modifying the game, you can change how they are placed and framed, just as you can with windows. Like windows, doors and entrances are a focal point of a building.

Choose an entranceway that matches or complements the build. For example, use formal, large entrances to castles, mansions, and city halls and smaller, cozier doorways for homes and village shops. The dark oak door object is suited to formal buildings and homes; the spruce door is perfect for farms and rustic builds; and the birch door suits casual, modern builds.

While you want to choose a door object that matches your building style, there are other features you can add to your entrance to make it unique. Here are several considerations that can help make your doorways unique and detailed.

Recess the door object

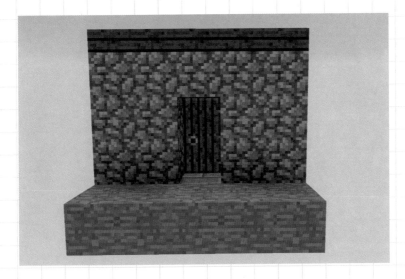

Place the door object so that it isn't flush with the walls around it, to add immediate depth.

Inset or bring out

Move your doorway in or out from the building.

Raise up

Raise the ground floor and doorway up and use steps to reach it.

Frames

Frame your entrance with contrasting blocks.

Layers

Add depth and layers with arches, columns, posts, porches, and eaves.

Paths

Adding a path or walkway to your door will bring visual focus to it.

More Doors and Entrances

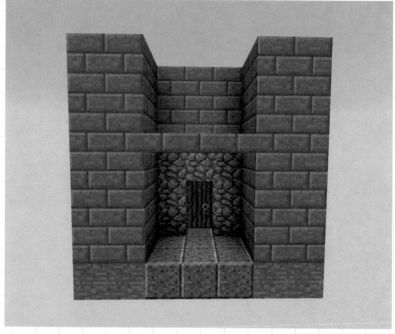

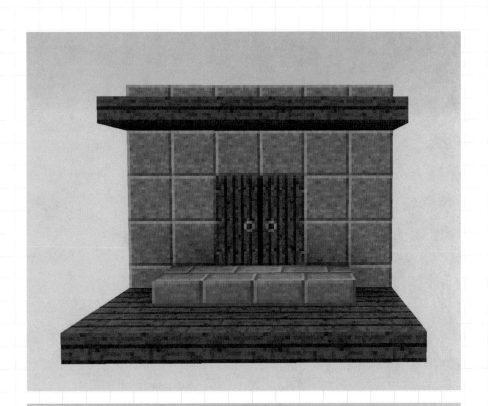

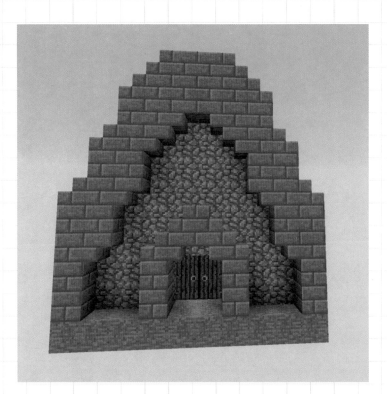

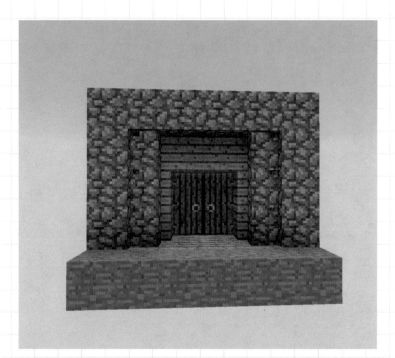

CHAPTER 5
ROOFS

ROOFS ARE PROBABLY THE MOST DIFFICULT PART OF building in *Minecraft*. The shape of your building can limit the type of roof you can add. Some roofs just can't be built properly above some shapes. When you start planning a build, it is a good idea to think about the roof, so that you can make sure the walls of your building will work with it.

One important part of planning a roof is deciding whether you want the peak of the roof to be one single block wide or two or more blocks wide. If you want the top ridge of your roof to be created by two stair blocks placed against each other, the building beneath will need to be an even number of blocks wide. If you do this, however, you won't be able to center a door in the wall below; you will need to use double doors if you want symmetry.

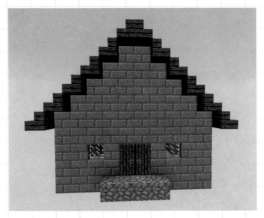

Roof ridge (center of roof) falls between two blocks. Two stairs can be used to create the ridge, and only double doors can be centered below. The front wall will need to be an even number of blocks wide.

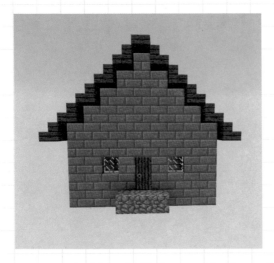

Roof ridge falls over a central block. Only one block can be used as the ridge, and a single door can be centered below. The front wall needs to be an odd number of blocks wide.

You will also want to plan the blocks, colors, and textures you'll be using for your roof. In almost all builds, you will want to build your roof from a different block than the block used for the walls. Following are some guidelines for making your roofs interesting and unique.

Contrast

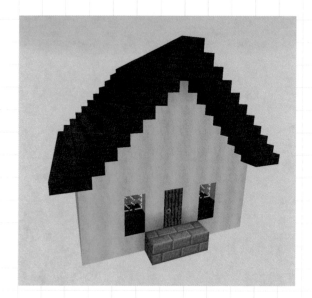

Use a block that contrasts with your walls.

Doubled stairs

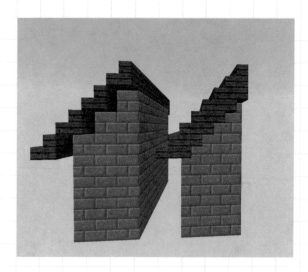

If you are using stairs for your wall, double them up. Place upside-down stairs next to the rising stair blocks to make the underside of the roof look like the topside.

Frames

Frame the roof, using a different block for edges and ridges.

Support braces

Add vertical strips of contrasting blocks, almost like external support braces, that break up long stretches of roof.

Pitch

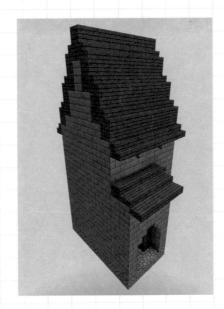

Use different slopes for different buildings, and even for different parts of the same building. For help in making steep or shallow roofs, and curved roofs, see the diagram "Roof Pitches."

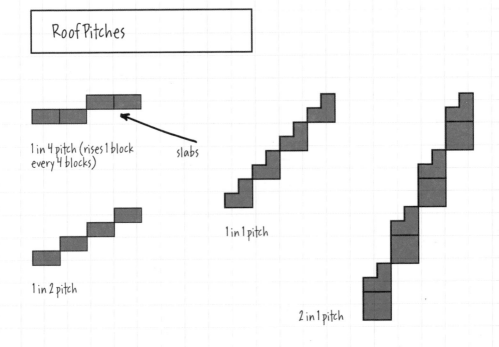

Roof Pitches

1 in 4 pitch (rises 1 block every 4 blocks)

slabs

1 in 1 pitch

1 in 2 pitch

2 in 1 pitch

Curves

Add curves and changing slopes (see diagram "Curved Roofs").

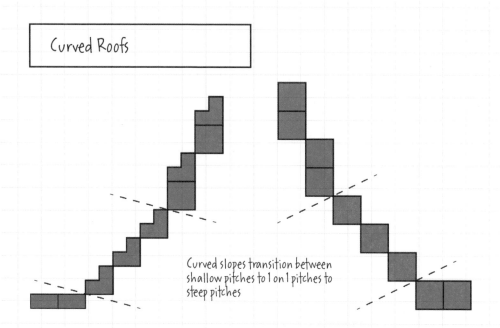

Curved Roofs

Curved slopes transition between
shallow pitches to 1 on 1 pitches to
steep pitches

Types of Roofs

There are many types of roofs in real life. Roofs that work well with *Minecraft*'s blocks and stairs include the following:

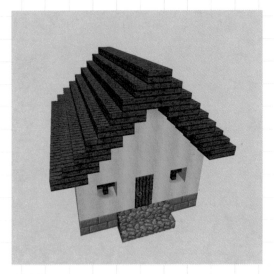

Gable

Stepped Gable

Hip

Intersecting Hip

Cross Hipped

Hip and Valley

Pyramid Hip

Gambrel

Flat

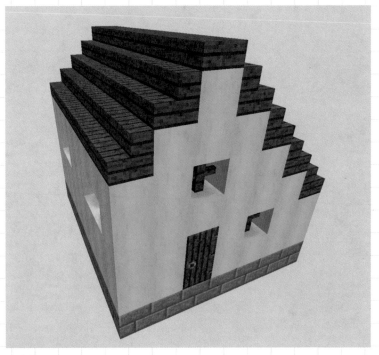

Saltbox

Shed

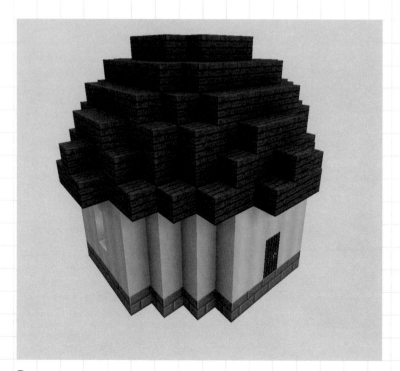

Dome

Onion Dome

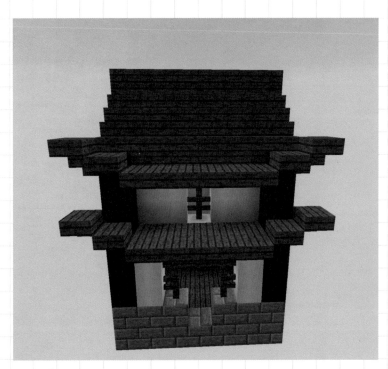

Pagoda

Sawtooth

M-Shaped

Barrel

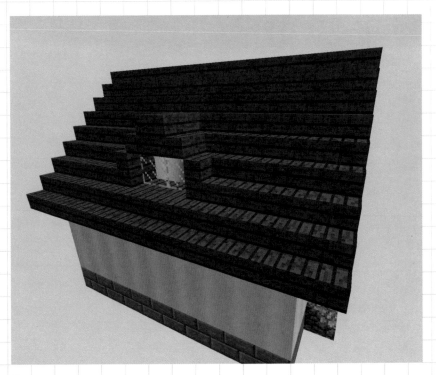

Dormer

Cupola

CHAPTER 6
STAIRS

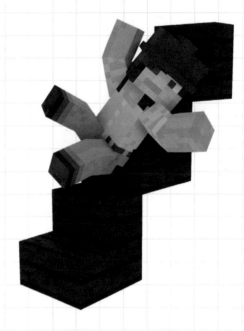

IN SMALL BUILDINGS, YOU OFTEN HAVE TO MAKE do with the simplest staircases, or even ladders, to move from floor to floor. There may not be enough space to allow many choices. However, with a little planning, you can use the staircase as another important element to convey your building's style and feel.

A key factor in your staircase is the distance it must rise. Of course, the distance between floors will dictate the number of blocks your staircase rises up. If you use stair blocks, this will be one block up per one block over. If you use slabs, this can be just one block up per two blocks over or less. When you plan your building, also plan where your staircases will go and how much room they will take up. If your staircase makes corners, a landing will add to the amount of space the stairs take up.

Ways to make your stairs stand out include the following:

Use two types of stair blocks

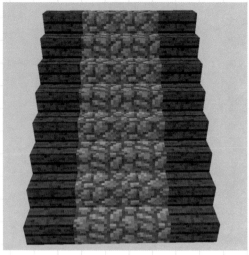

Use contrasting or complementary stairs together. With wider staircases, 3 blocks or wider, use different stair blocks at the edges to bring visual interest and definition.

Landings and turns

The classic, straight staircase is called a straight-run staircase. Add interest and variety to your build by using landings to change the stairs' direction.

Use different blocks

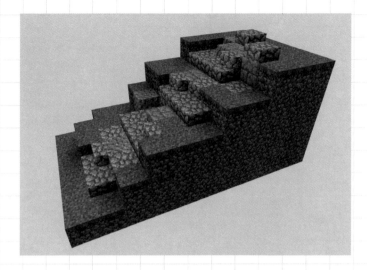

If your stairs are outdoors and casual or rustic, you can use slabs and blocks in place of some of the stair blocks to make the steps look uneven and dilapidated.

Use railings

Use fences and/or blocks as railings.

Use posts

Break up long stretches of railings with regular posts.

Building a Curved Staircase

ONE OF THE EASIEST WAYS TO BUILD A CURVED STAIRCASE IS TO FIRST BUILD CIRCLES TO GUIDE THE CURVE. BUILD THE CIRCLE OUT TO BE AS WIDE AS THE STAIRCASE WILL BE (THIS SHOULD BE AT LEAST 3 WIDE). THEN USE SLABS TO BUILD THE CIRCLE UP INTO RISING STEPS.

Types of Stairs

Straight run

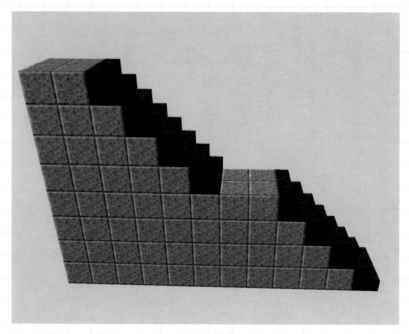

Straight two-flight stair with half-landing

Quarter-turn stair with landing

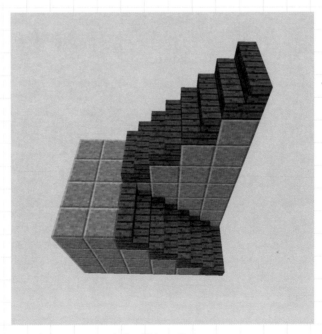

Dogleg stair with half-landing

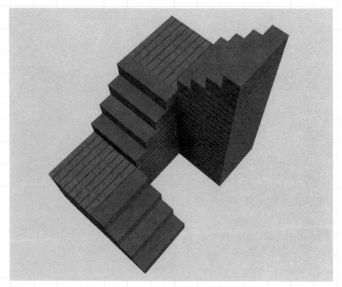

Open well stair with two quarter landings (three-quarter-turn stair)

Spiral stair with central column

CHAPTER 7
PATHS AND ROADS

ROADS AND PATHS ARE ALMOST COMPLETELY UNNECESSARY IN *Minecraft*—for gameplay. You can fly with your Elytra or race directly over rocky terrain without a problem. For immersion—feeling as if you are really in a new world—roads and paths can be a key element in creating your world. Whether it's a trail that leads you to a distant village, paths that take you to the river where you fish, or interconnected city streets, a road will make your builds and favorite locations more meaningful and give them more visual interest and attention. Making different roads unique—so that they are not all three-block-wide cobble strips—will also make your buildings and destinations unique.

Building tactics to make your roads and paths unique include the following:

Contrast

Add contrast by using blocks with different textures and colors. Using blocks that are very similar, like gravel and andesite, can give a surface a distinct textured look.

Detail

Add borders to roads; add sidewalks, gutters, streetlights, benches, traffic lights, pedestrian crossings, and trees to city streets; add hedges and short walls lining country roads.

Movement

Although many modern cities and highways have long stretches of straight roads, your own roads in *Minecraft* tend to look much better with curves, rises, and drops. So, add movement with curves— occasionally turning left or right and/or moving up and down slight hills. Where you can, use the landscape: follow the curve of a river and rise of a hill.

Types of roads and paths

When building your roads, think about their purpose as this can help give you an idea of the type of road you want. City buildings will usually be located on streets, while a mansion might be situated along an avenue. Types of roads and paths include the following:

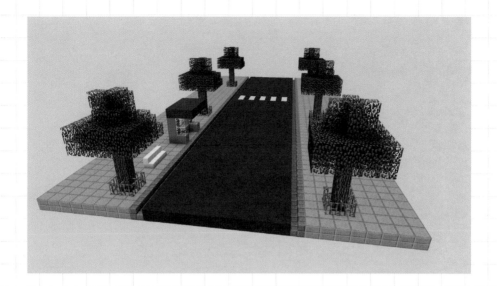

Street

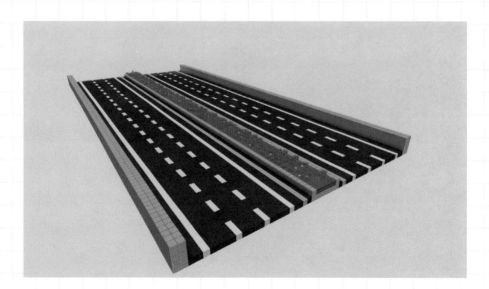

Highway

Country roads

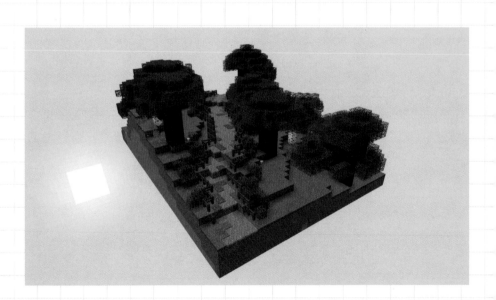

Bridle paths

Footpaths

Garden paths

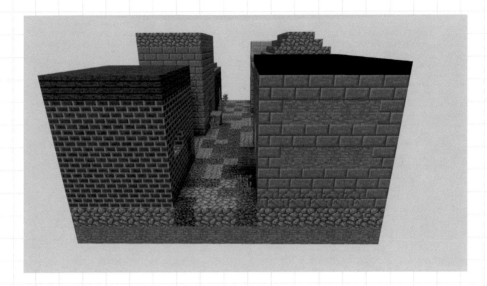

Alleys

Boulevards

Dirt roads

Avenues

Road palettes

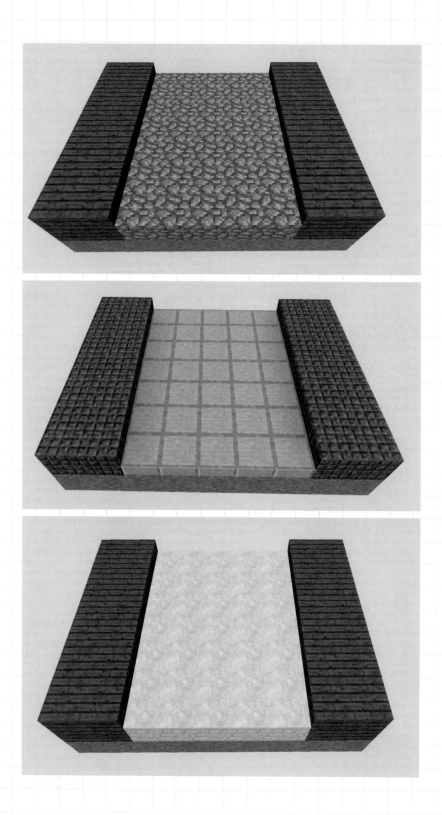

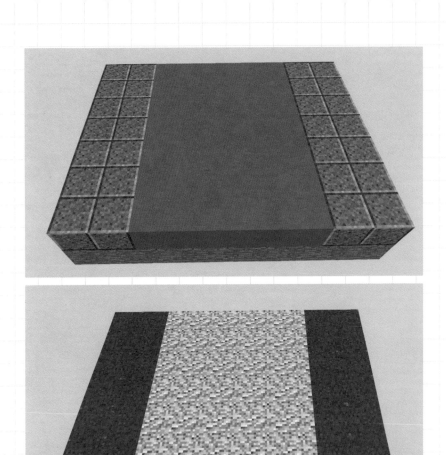

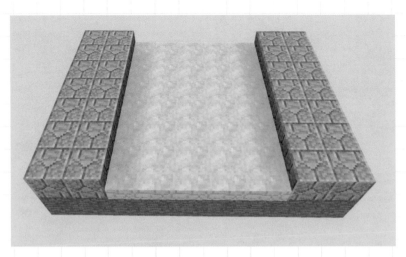

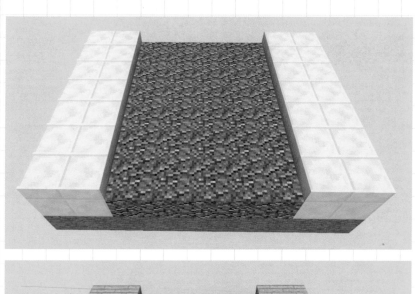

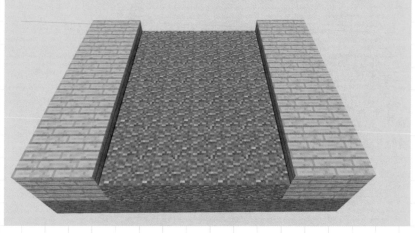

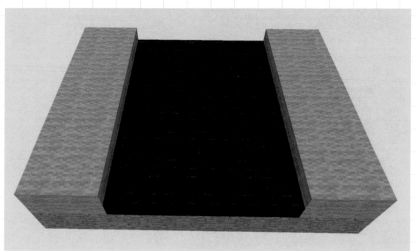

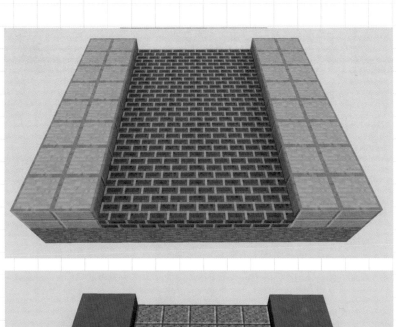

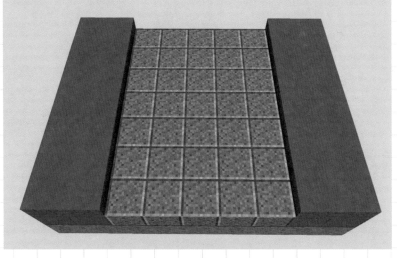

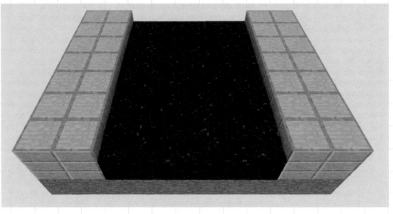

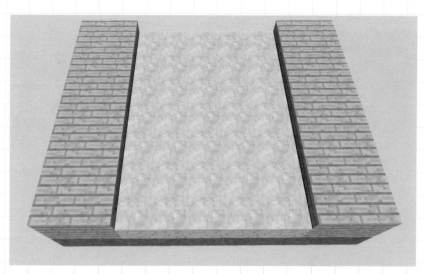

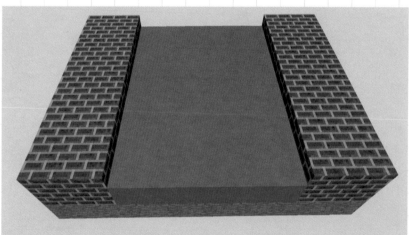

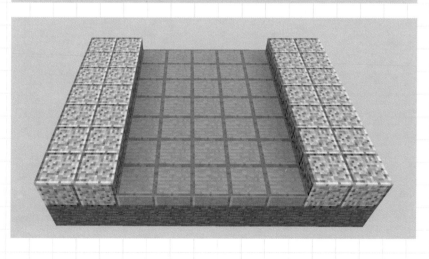

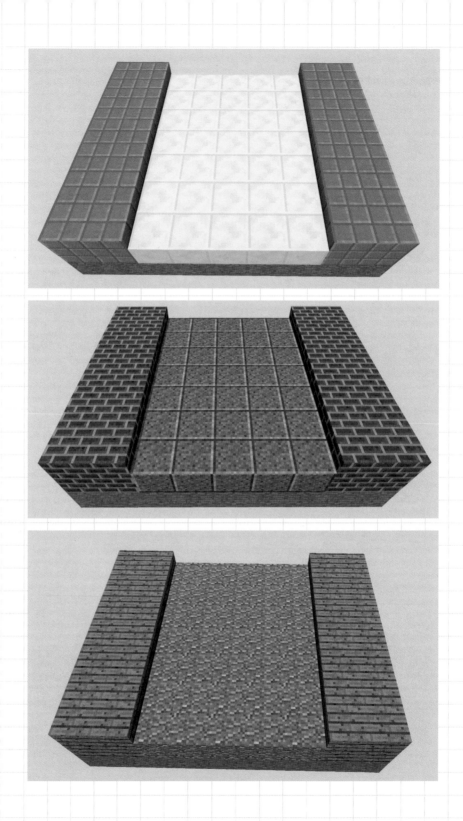

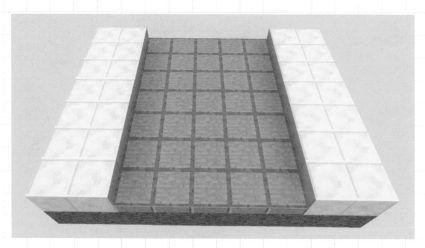

CHAPTER 8
BRIDGES

LIKE ROADS, BRIDGES ARE A GREAT WAY TO add to the immersion of playing in your world; giving you the feeling that it is a real place you are living in. In the real world, you'd probably avoid swimming across the river and choose a bridge instead! Although building bridges is a bit similar to creating roads, bridges are a bit more difficult. They tend to look best when the bridge is curved. If you create a straight bridge, over a mountain pass for example, it will often be more interesting if you can add curved features like arches.

Bridge Features

As with other *Minecraft* builds, you can make your bridges more interesting by breaking up flat surfaces. With a straight-beam bridge, you'll probably want to add features like columns, railings, and other details to give it character. Features to consider adding to your bridge include the following:

Support

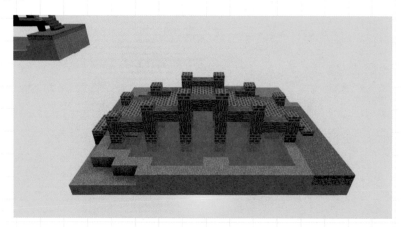

Add simple or detailed support columns below your bridge, leaving room for boats to pass through, if you want. Of course, you aren't limited to columns for bridge support. You can use walls of arches or even a single wall running beneath the bridge.

Arches

You can use arches with or in place of support columns to support your bridge. Arches can be shallow or steep, although in general, the wider the arch, the more the top of the arch will look like a curve. Look also to the section on Arches on page 124 for different shapes and styles of arches.

Railings and posts

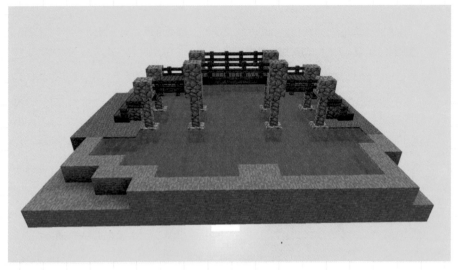

Add railings and short walls above the road bed with fences, bars, and gates. Break stretches of railing up with regularly spaced posts. Space posts so that they complement any support columns.

Contrasting blocks

Use contrasting blocks in the center of the road bed. You may also want to use contrasting blocks for support columns, trusses, posts, or arches.

Slope and curves

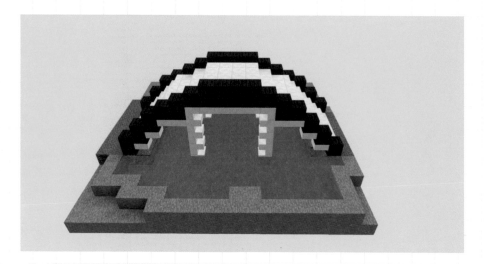

How high above the river or pass will your bridge rise? You can use a steep slope, using stairs, or a slower rise, using slabs.

Roofs

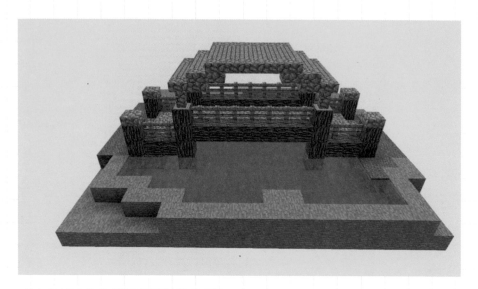

A fully or partially covered roof can give a bridge an old-time or protected feel.

Types of Bridges

Because gravity isn't a concern for building in *Minecraft*, you can build any type of crossing—a bridge doesn't have to be supported by beams or suspension trusses. But if realism is a goal, look to real-life bridge types as a guide for the basic form and shape of your bridge. There are many types of bridges in real life. Three bridge types that adapt well to the blocks of *Minecraft* include:

Beam bridge

A beam bridge is supported by vertical beams. A simple log over a river is a beam bridge.

Arch bridge

An arch bridge is supported by arches beneath the bridge or may use an arch itself as the bridge. A Roman aqueduct, built to transport water, is a type of arched bridge.

Truss bridge

A truss bridge uses a series of interconnected supports, often in triangles, to hold the road bed (the part you walk over). The road bed may be at the top of the trusses, at the bottom, or in the middle.

You don't have to be confined to replicating these types of bridges. Fantasy bridges may need no support, or you can create unique types of support for your bridges. You can make casual bridges from slabs and fences.

Designing a Bridge

Before you begin building, first make sure that both ends of the bridge will be at the same height and that they are also directly opposite each other.

If you want your bridge to look symmetrical, measure the distance the bridge will travel over the river or gap. You want arches and columns to be spaced evenly or similarly spaced on the left and right sides of the bridge. Find the exact center of the gap you are building over. This will help figure out spacing, as you want the same number of features (columns, arches, decorations, gaps) on one side of the center as the other.

You also want the bridge to begin at approximately the same distance from the river bank on either side. Once you have the measure of the river, you can figure out how many pillars or arches will fit. You can use temporary blocks or even lily pads to show where your columns or arches will go and where the bridge will start on the sides of the river.

At the same time, decide how long the middle of the bridge will be and how high above the ground. The higher the bridge is, the longer the rise to the middle will need to be. If you are working in Survival mode, using grid paper can help with planning a large bridge. You can also use temporary, easy-to-break blocks, like dirt or wool, to show the basic form of the bridge.

Building an arched bridge:

1. First measure the span you are crossing and find the center.

2. Determine how far below the center you want the top of the central arch to be.

3. Build out the shape of the central arch below this point.

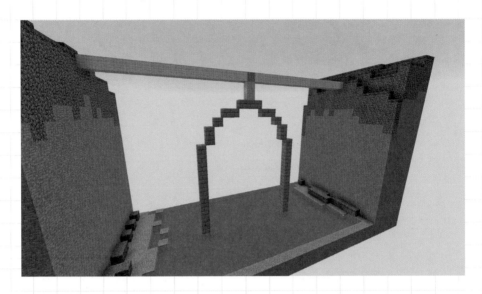

4. Build out the shape of any arches that you want to the side.

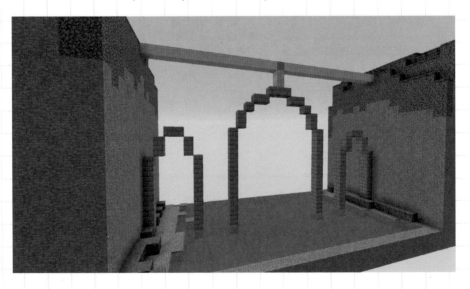

5. Fill in the wall.

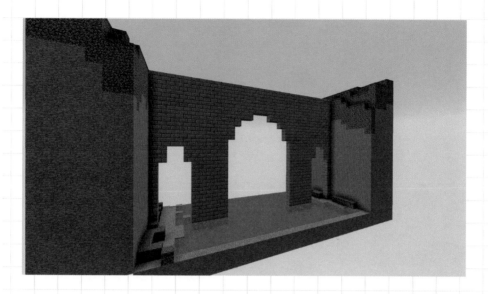

6. Use stairs and slabs to soften the curve of the arch.

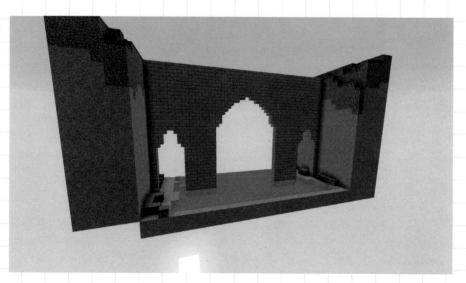

7. Build the arched wall out to be as wide as you want the bridge: here, it is five blocks wide.

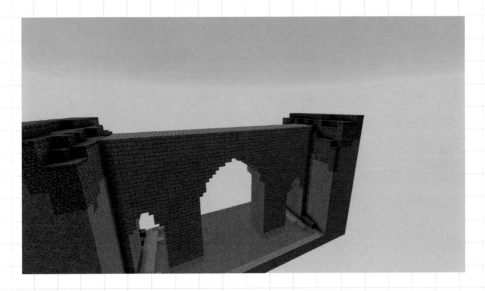

8. Now the shape is done, it's time to add details. Here, I've punched out two shapes between the arches and filled in the inner blocks as cobblestone.

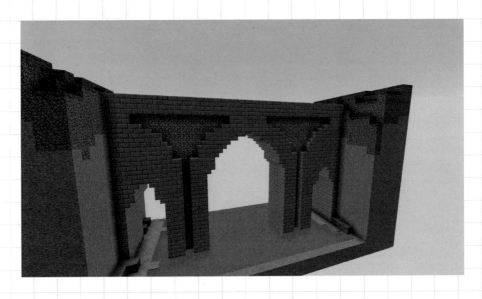

9. Above the road bed, I've added a lip a block high of stone brick and added crenellations of cobble above these short walls.

10. Finally, I've added stone slabs to the stalk of the inset designs. Bridge complete!

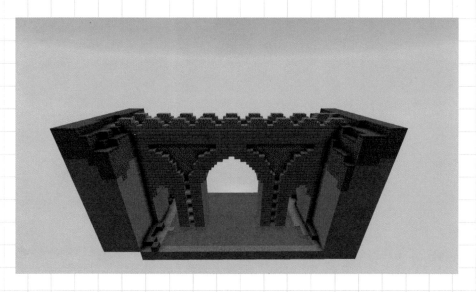

More Bridges

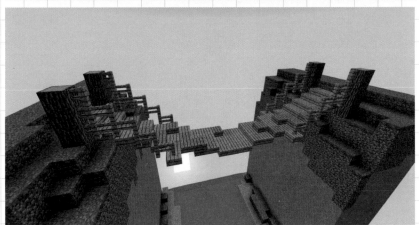

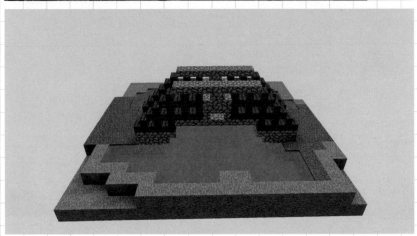

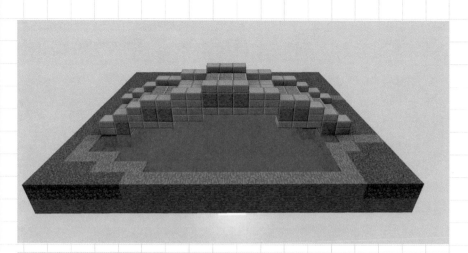

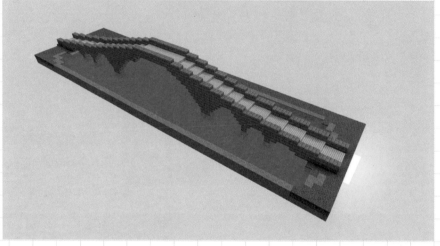

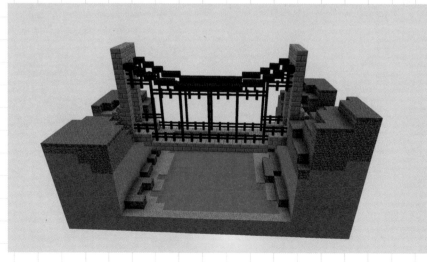

CHAPTER 9
PALETTES

IF YOU ARE STUCK PICKING OUT BLOCKS FOR your build, developing palettes can help. A palette is a selection of colors that work well together. In *Minecraft*, it's a selection of blocks that work well together. For a big build, you'll want the following types of blocks in your palette:

1. A block that has stair and slab versions.

2. One to three main blocks that are used for the bulk of the structure.

3. One or two highlight blocks that provide contrast in color or texture to the main blocks.

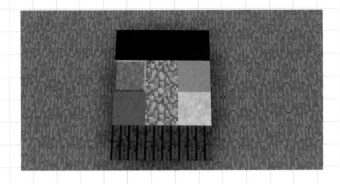

When you create a palette, look for blocks that share tones. The blocks in *Minecraft* often have multiple color tints; for example, prismarine bricks have yellowish-greenish pixels, changing to purplish, as well as aqua. If you are looking for blocks that work well with prismarine, you can start with blocks that also have yellow/green or purple tints. When you've picked out a few blocks that go together, put them side by side for a look at how they work together.

Inspiration for color palettes can come from many places, including looking at other *Minecrafters'* builds, nature, paint swatches, photographs, illustrations, paintings, clothing, and magazines. Here are some sample four-block palettes to look through if you get stuck. Not all include the types of blocks listed above, and some very colorful samples are more suited to fantasy builds than realistic builds. However, the combinations and textures shown here may inspire you to choose blocks or colors you hadn't considered for your build, or give you an idea for an entirely different selection of blocks and colors.

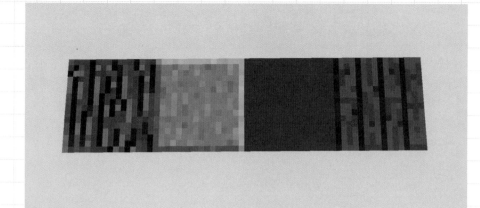

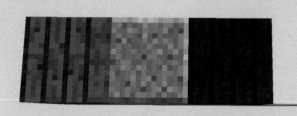

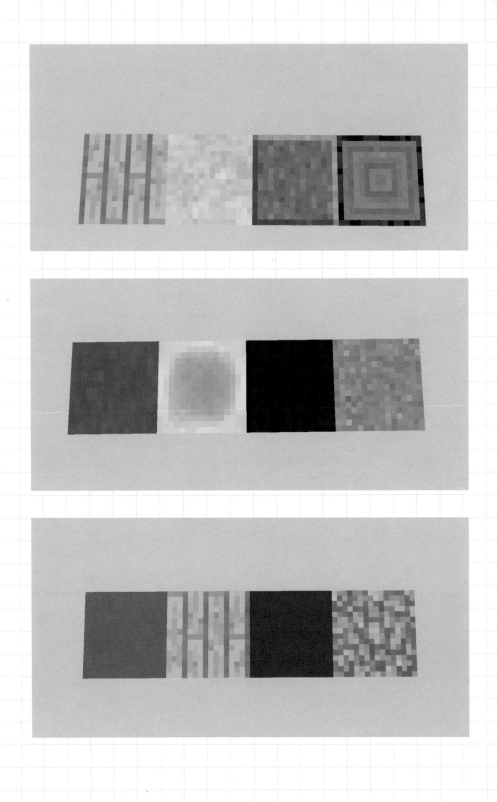

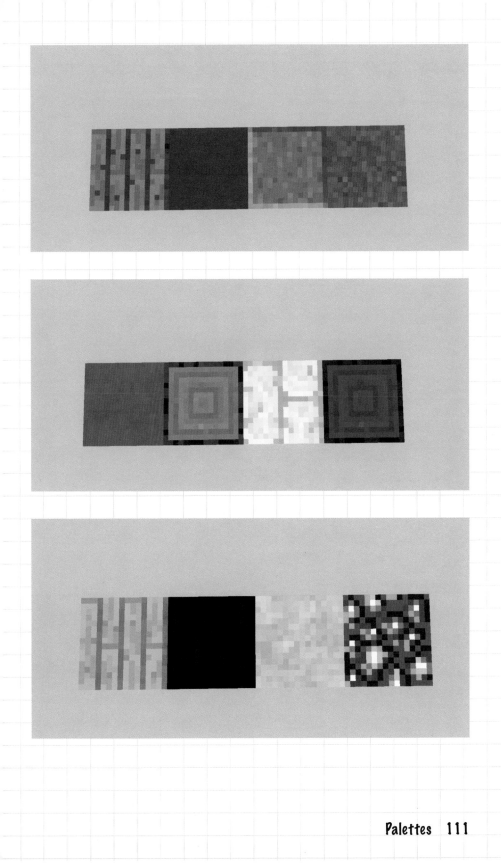

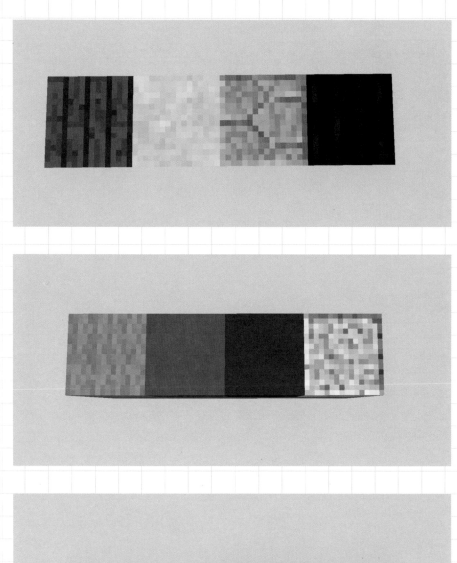

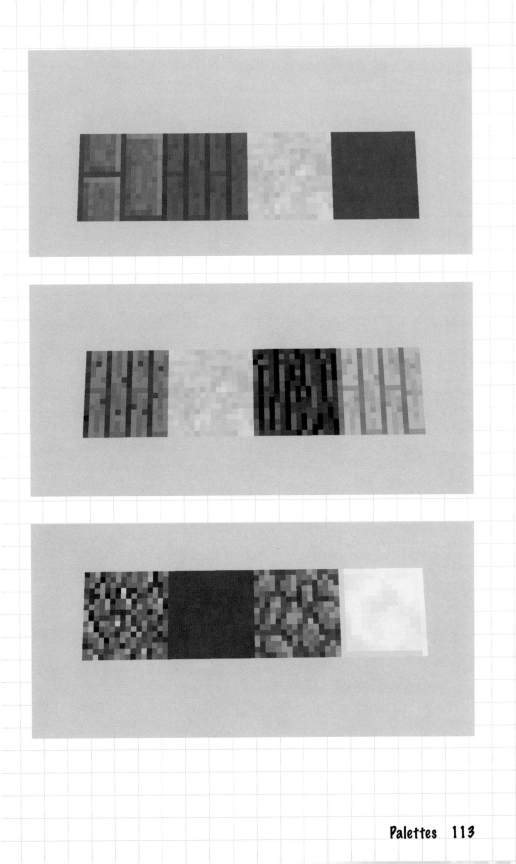

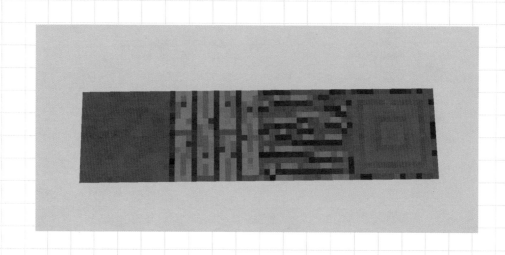

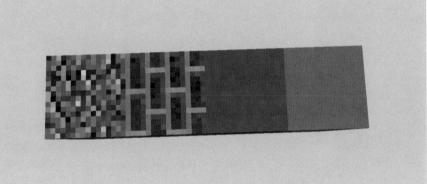

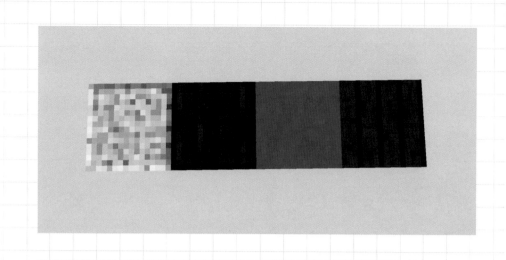

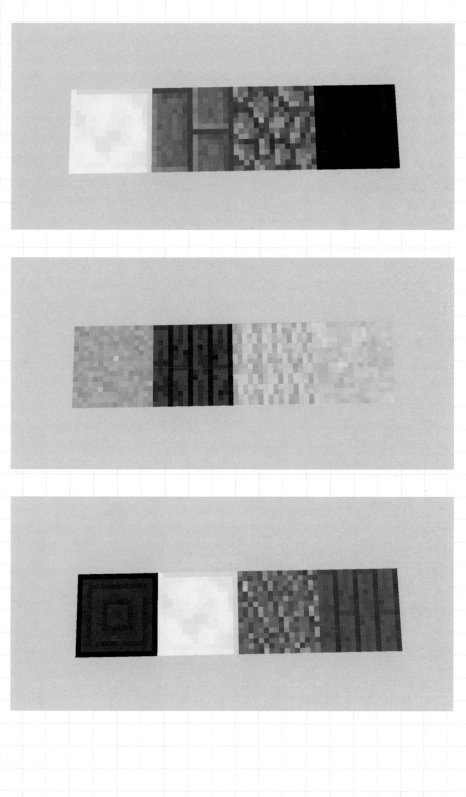

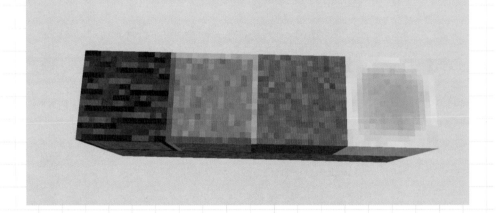

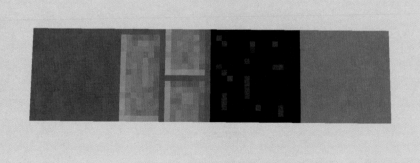

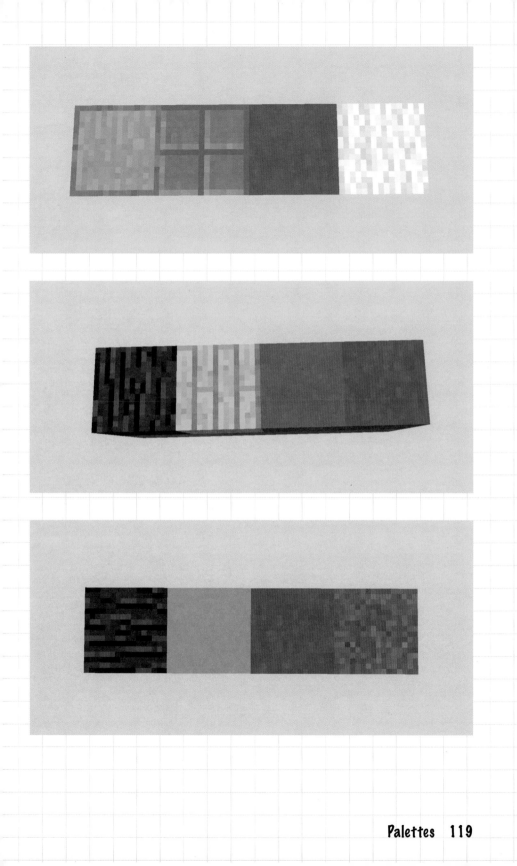

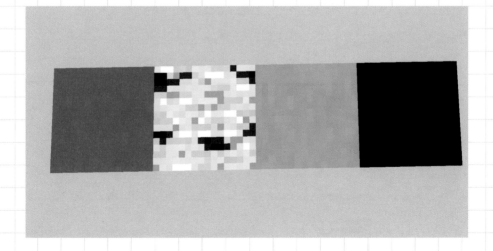

CHAPTER 10
OTHER ARCHITECTURAL FEATURES

WINDOWS, WALLS, ROOFS, AND STAIRS ARE THE BIG features of a building, but there are a number of other architectural features and details that you can add to buildings to make them unique or to further add to the building's look and feel.

Arches

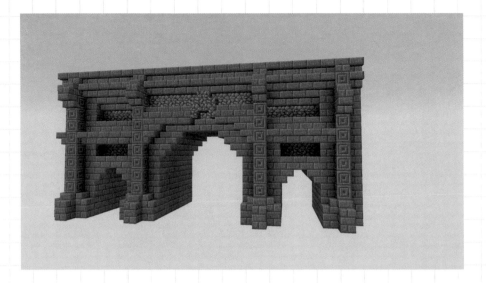

Arches can be used for bridge supports, triumphal arches, as frames for doors and windows, and as gateways in protective walls. The trick in building an arch is in creating the curved or circular shape at the top of the arch. There are many types of arches; a few that work well with *Minecraft* are in the diagram "Types of Arches." To help construct different and larger shapes of arches, you can also search online for *Minecraft* arch templates, which also show how to place each block.

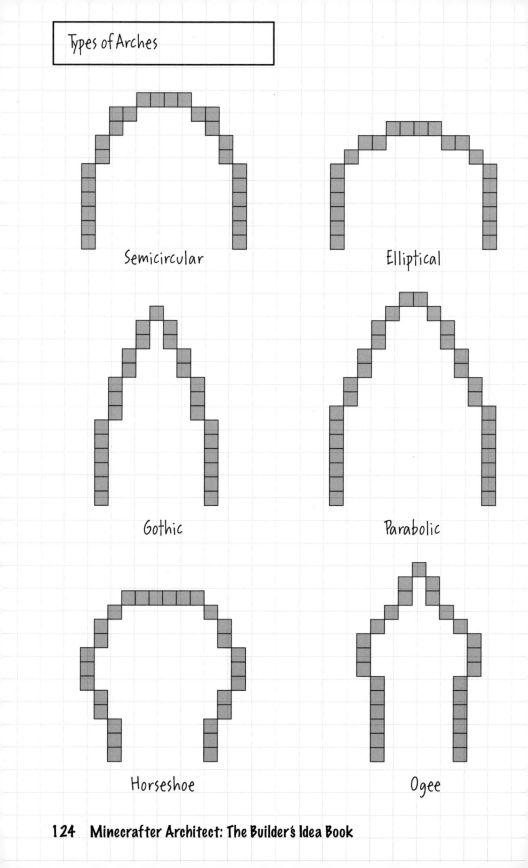

Types of Arches

Semicircular

Elliptical

Gothic

Parabolic

Horseshoe

Ogee

Balconies

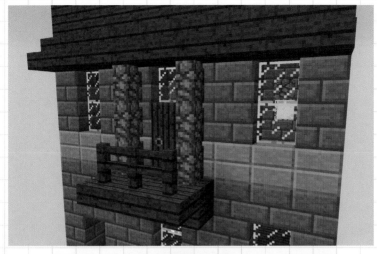

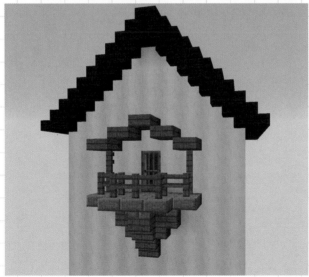

Balconies add lots of details to homes and buildings. They can also be a pleasant lookout from which to shoot mobs at night. When you are adding a balcony to a building, use a contrasting block to the main building block so that the balcony stands out. Adding supports beneath the balcony will also add a touch of detail and realism.

Buttresses

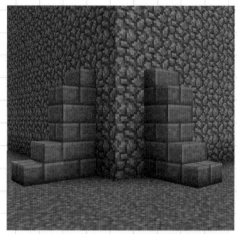

Clockwise from top left: angle buttress, set-back buttress, flying buttress, clasping buttress

Buttresses are shallow walls designed to reinforce large structures, and you will find them on old cathedrals and castles. They are a great detail to add in your larger buildings.

Chimneys

Add chimneys to roofs of homes and older buildings and factories. With smaller homes or workplaces, the chimney can extend out from the wall of the house as it travels down to its fireplace. If you do add chimneys, you don't also have to add fireplaces or chimney flues! One block wide chimneys suit smaller homes, while bigger edifices and factories can have 2x2 chimneys without looking unbalanced.

Columns

Columns are a popular way to add detail to *Minecraft* builds. You can use them to support or decorate arches, doorways, entranceways, porticos, porches, and as support for majestic ceilings. You can use stair blocks and contrasting blocks to make them stand out.

Foundations

In real life, foundations are the base support for a building and are usually made of concrete or masonry (bricks and mortar). Their purpose is to provide strength and stability to the building. In *Minecraft*, you can add contrast and detail by creating a foundation for the first one or two rows of your house and raising the door up to accommodate that.

Make Your Own Idea Book

As you continue on your adventure of creative Minecraft building, you may want to keep a record or an album of images of buildings and other inspiring sights. You can download images to your own computer folders, keep a scrapbook, or use an online image curation service like Pinterest to collect your favorite images.

Don't limit your collection to just buildings: Colorful images from nature, patterns you see, artists' paintings, and anything you find interesting visually could be a source of inspiration to you.

As you build, also think of what people who live in your buildings might need. Will they need a garden where they can plant flowers, a fenced area to raise rabbits, or a protective wall to keep their shelter safe?

Think like an architect and enjoy creating!